Love is in the air

A collection of love poems

Other Books by the Author

Thoughts from a Faraway Place, a collection of poetry (2021)
  ISBN 978-1-7884824-1-7
Spid the Spider Has a Day Off (2021)
  ISBN 978-1-9996698-5-0
Spid the Spider Battles a Pandemic (2021)
  ISBN 978-1-9996698-1-2
Spid the Spider Goes to the Moon (Feb 2022)
  ISBN 978-1-9996698-7-4
Spid the Spider Visits the Seven Wonders of the World (Mar 2022)
  ISBN 978-19996698-8-1
Spid the Spider Helps Out at Spidmas (May 2022)
  ISBN 978-19996698-4-3
Spid the Spider Gets Spooked at Halloween (Sept 2022)
  ISBN 978-1-915376-00-8
Spid the Spider Welcomes in the New Year (Nov 2022)
  ISBN 978-1-915376-03-9
Spid the Spider Plans a Birthday Surprise (April 2023)
  ISBN 978-1-915376-09-1
Spid the Spider Goes on Holiday (July 2023)
  ISBN 978-1-915376-12-1
Spid the Spider Helps Save the Planet (Sept 2023)
  ISBN 978-191537-6-06-0
Spid the Spider Joins Sir Francis Duck and His Pirates (July 2024)
  ISBN 978-1-915376-18-3.
Spid the Spider Investigates a Mystery at Easter (Feb 2024) ISBN 978-191537-6-15-2
Spid the Spider Meets Hamish McSpid (Nov 2024)
  ISBN 978-191537-6-21-3
Don't Forget to Flush, poems that will drive you clean around the bend, (Dec 2024) ISBN 978-1915376-91-6

Albums by the Author

I'm Having Fun, Spid the Spider (2020) 06091158003
The Fun Goes On, Spid the Spider (2021) 0796548139592
For Julia and Ukraine, various artists (2022) 0796548016497
Under Ukrainian Skies, various artists (2023) 0796548618226
Tomorrow Begins Today, various artists (2023) 0781005393365
Fun, Fun, Fun, Spid the Spider (Sept 2024) 0604565870810

Love is in the air

A collection of love poems

John Eaton

Copyright © John Eaton 2025. All rights reserved.

ISBN 978-1-915376-97-8 (Paperback)

ISBN 978-1-915376-98-5 (Epub)

Published by Spidling Productions Ltd, Meadow Court, Minehead Road, Taunton, Somerset, TA2 6NS, England

No part of this publication may be reproduced, stored in a retrieval system or transmitted in any form or by any means, electronic, mechanical, photocopying, recording, scanning or otherwise except under the terms of the Copyright, Designs and Patents Act 1988 or under terms of a licence issued by the Copyright Licensing Agency, 5th Floor, Shackleton House, 4 Battle Bridge Lane, London, SE1 2HX, England, without the permission in writing of the publisher.

British Library Cataloguing in Publication Data

A catalogue reference for this book is available from the British Library.

Cover by Julia Vasina

Typeset by Shakspeare Editorial

To lovers and romantics everywhere

CONTENTS

♪ = also a song, use QR code

Preface	xi
Valentine One	1
No Doubt	2
I Can't Get Enough Of You ♪	3
You	5
Coward In Love	6
Timeless Love	7
Decision Time	8
Flowers	10
In Seine Love	11
I'm Not Walking Away ♪	12
Naughty But Nice	14
Long Distance Call	15
Card Shock	17
Looking	18
Colour Blind	19
Love Mist ♪	20
Postcard	22
Love On The Lake	23
Shaky Love	25
Love, Children And Life	26
Forbidden Love	27
Valentine Surprise	28
Flo	30
Bray	31

Love Tribute	32
Come Back	33
Oh Joy	34
Marriage?	36
My Valentine's Choice	37
Postbox	38
What?	39
Love ♪	40
A Bard's Reply	42
Gone	44
True Love	45
May I Ask You Your Name?	46
Hidden Love	47
Valentine Girl	48
Love Bites	50
Wow, Wow, She Loves Me ♪	51
Togetherness	54
Love A-Plenty	56
Braille	57
Empty	58
How To Make A Valentine Cake	59
Ballentine Valentine	61
Spice Up Your Life	62
Kiss	63
My Valentine	64
The Love–Hate Game	65
Valentine's Jest	67

February Frolics	68
Whoopie!	69
St Valentine's Night	70
Love Is Like A Cardboard Box	72
St Valentine's Massacre	73
Notice	75
Neighbour	76
Love Is An Open Door ♪	77
Nameless	79
Communicate	80
Oh Darling	81
A Young Man From Liskeard	82
Valentino	83
I Wish	84
Painful	85
Goodbye	86
Love Is A Four-Letter Word ♪	87
E-Card	89
I Love You	91
Only You	92
Waiting For Love	93
Try A Little Tinderness	94
Priceless	95
Our Song	96
Love Birds	97
Certain Nothing	98
Work And Play	99

Old Croc	100
Little By Little	101
I'm Looking Out For You ♪	102
Crypto	105
Hot Love	106
Rolo Love	107
Fantastic	108
Explaining	109
Everything	110
Spring Love	111
Owed To Love ♪	112
Tomorrow	114
I Dream	115
Missing You	116
I Just Want You To Stay ♪	117
Warmly	119
Coined	120
My Love	121
Song For Love ♪	122
Saying	124
My Friend ♪	125
No Problem	127
Petal	128
About the Author	130

PREFACE

The Beatles sang 'All you need is love'.
They also say love makes the world go round, and as the world turns on its axis twenty-four hours a day, that means love is all around all of the time.
It is a wonderful feeling to fall in love and be loved back. And I hope that feeling applies to you.
This collection of poems tries to capture the feelings of pleasure, poignancy and pain about love. The poems cover different occasions, places and people:
- ♥ Boys loving girls and vice versa
- ♥ Parents loving their children and vice versa
- ♥ Grandchildren cherishing their grandparents and vice versa
- ♥ Same gender lover between men and between women
- ♥ The love we feel for our closest friends and loyal pets.

Love is something that comes from within and can be sparked by a glance across a room, a friendly word, a caring gesture. Some say by 'je ne sais quoi'.
The source is for you to know and feel. So, as you read this book of love poems, remember that someone loves you.

Some of these poems are also songs. To hear (and see music videos) of some of the songs just scan the accompanying QR codes. Please note that there may be small differences between the poems and the song lyrics.

So, relax, read, sometimes listen to, and enjoy these Valentine love thoughts.

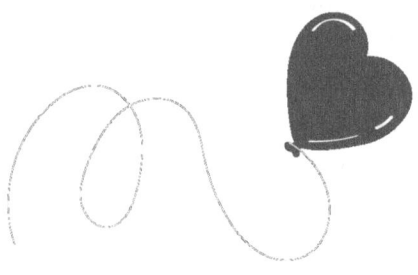

VALENTINE ONE

This is my first Valentine's card
Sent to me by someone j'adore
And thus far I can describe and believe
Because my feelings are for all to see.

But who is this suitor?
A friend, a colleague, a tutor
With an eye on my impending future?
Though if I guess who it is, it's only rumour.
I then check the envelope
In case there is a message for us to elope.

Suddenly, I recall who sent this tiny tome.
It was me, sent anonymously to myself
Ensuring my Valentine's heart would melt.

NO DOUBT

You are so beautiful
Gorgeous and dutiful
As solid as a crucible
All this is irrefutable.

I CAN'T GET ENOUGH OF YOU

I can't get enough of you.
I can't get enough of you.
What, what can I do?
Help me, help me, help me.

No matter what I do.
No matter what I do.
I have tried.
You know that I have tried.

I don't know where to go.
The only thing I know
    is that I'm in love with you.

I can't get enough of you.
I can't get enough of you.
What, what can I do?
Help me, help me, help me.

No matter what I do.
No matter what I do.
I have tried; you know that I have tried.

I don't know where to go.
The only thing I know
    is that I'm in love with you.

How can I explain to you
    the feelings that I have?
And they are all true.
I'm in love with you. With you.

When will you come to me?
You're the only one for me.
But you are with another
    and she is your child's mother.

So, I must turn away
And see you another day.
It will always have to be this way.

I Can't Get Enough of You

YOU

You love me. You love me not.
You leave me cold. You leave me hot.
You build me up. You shoot me down.
I would not know what to do if you were not
　around.

COWARD IN LOVE

Today is the day
That I'm allowed to say
With all my heart and soul –
And when I say it, I'm on a roll.

Perhaps with flowers?
Also, a card, some perfume
And champagne to consume.
To while away the hours.

I'll shave and shower
And be ready in an hour.
I'll meet you for a meal
To tell you how I feel.

But as I splash the aftershave all over,
I get a cold feeling on my shoulder.
I will duck my first date.
Leaving our love to fate.

TIMELESS LOVE

I know that I am in love
With someone sent from above
Someone who will mind me gently.
Someone I will stay with to eternity.

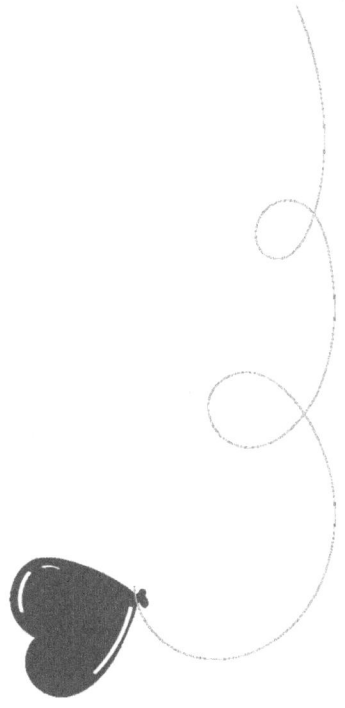

DECISION TIME

Oh, the pain of love.
A word that tugs on my heart.
I don't really know how to start.
Love is the word that is tearing me apart.
Like having a horse while others have a cart.

You love me. Is this true?
I haven't a clue.
I wonder what you would say on our wedding day.
I only hope it is 'I do'.

I feel so happy, yet so sad.
In good faith and with bad.
How can you love someone so much
Yet don't get a response from a touch?

I'm falling into a rabbit hole of emotion
Full of unrequited love and devotion.
Yet, whatever gave me the notion
That a drop of water makes an ocean?

Don't you know how I feel?
Oh, how my heart creaks at the wheel?
I give so much and get so little in return
It's not surprising that I have my concerns.

In life, there are times when we have to choose
Between going forward in your own voice
Or staying behind and missing the choice.
A wrong decision will change your future;
To make me either a winner or a loser.

FLOWERS

Roses are red, violets are blue,
Primroses are yellow, tulips are green –
Unless they are not, which may be true,
Depending on the bouquet's variety of genes.

IN SEINE LOVE

Meet me in Paris on February 14.
Valentine's Day in the City of Love.
Bring me a ring to embrace.
Let us forever make love in this place.

Bring me a lock,
    so we can take stock
    of our love for each other.

We can have fun
    in the spring morning sun,
    with you alone as my lover.

Meet me on the bridge by Notre Dame.
We can lock our love there
And throw the key into the river.
Kiss, then go to dinner.

To ensure our love is on the altar,
Knowing we will never falter.
Understanding we will never need to explain.
Our love was not abridged, but insane.

I'M NOT WALKING AWAY

Another time, another day,
I would think of another way.
Emotions take the floor.
I would walk out of the door.

But then I'd stop and think
    of the times we've been on the brink
    of losing everything we had.
I never ever want to come to that.

So, I'm not walking away.
I'll stay all night and day
I'll fight for our love
    even if, at times, it's been tough.

Of everything we've had,
    in happiness and sad,
    we've taken it all together.
Memories we share forever.

And yes, we quarrel late at night.
We square up but do not fight.
We respect each other's place
    understanding we all make mistakes.

So, I'm not walking away.
I'll stay all night and day
I'll fight for our love
    even if, at times, it's been tough.

I wake up another day.
More problems will come our way.
We'll get through them one by one
Until all of them have gone.

I look around and see
    others who are just like us.
They break up without a fuss
because they fail to discuss.

So, I say to you,
Don't walk away.
Stay all night and all day.
You need to fight for your love.

Walking away is not enough.
Walking away is not enough.
Walking away is not enough.
Walking away is not enough.
Walking away is not enough.

I'm Not Walking Away

NAUGHTY BUT NICE

Could it be you are the one for me?
Opening my mind and setting it free.
Freeing me from the mess in my head.
I can't wait to get you into bed.

LONG DISTANCE CALL

I phoned my love from Sydney
It was a second past midnight
I was hoping that you might
Pick up the phone with delight

I hoped you'd rejoice
On hearing my voice
In a one-to-one call
You'd have no choice.

The line we were on
Was particularly poor
Like an emergency call
From ship to shore.

You thought I called you lazy
And was phoning from Paisley.
That I was trying to avoid
And you were getting annoyed.

So I wished you a great Valentine's Day!
What else could I say?
That was the reason for the call.
You said, 'Are you mad, or not on the ball?
In the UK, it's the 13th of February,
I think you've lost your memory.'

You said, 'Call me tomorrow.
Even if you call from Chicago,
when it's Valentine's Day here.
Then you will do it on the right day, in the right year.
So if you don't mind, and I'm going to be clear,
Wipe out your ears and listen to my thunder
Then hang up as you've rung the wrong number.'

CARD SHOCK

I came home from work at breakfast time
There was a card on the floor, odour from Calvin
 Klein.
I opened it up
Couldn't believe my luck.
My love had sent me a Valentine!

LOOKING

Loneliness is the longest word,
    of the many thoughts that bring me hurt.
Valentine's Day makes me sad,
    eating alone in my one-bedroom pad.

Alone, alone, alone
Like a dog without a bone
A tramp without a home
Or a writer whose lost their tome.

Away from love
I pray to the above
For us to become
Two instead of one.

I wish for a dish
Good looks and a smile
Or just to be tidy for a while.
For you to want me with my ways,
Along a journey on love's highways.

I'll settle for less
Not what I want, I guess.
Just as long as I discover
That we can love one another.

COLOUR BLIND

Black is black. White is white.
Colours add vistas to make life bright.
It doesn't matter what colours you find,
With our love, I'm colour blind.

LOVE MIST

If you fall in love
Look to the sky.
Gauge the light
To make sure it's bright.

It may be its glow is not so bright
That will hit you like a stone fall!
Ask yourself why?
Find another way.
Try.

Love is a feeling that cannot be felt.
Its heat may be stifling
But its glaciers don't melt.
It will always leave you smiling.

If you touch love, but it is there.
If you see it but deny it if you dare.
You cannot hear it, though it's in the air.
You smell it, it's the zest from everywhere.

Love is in the ether
You can't measure it on a meter
It can't be hit by a missile
It can't be heard like a whistle
Or prick you like a thistle

Love is a feeling that cannot be felt.
Its heat may be stifling
But its glaciers don't melt.
It will always leave you smiling.

Love causes your heart to race.
You sweat profusely, especially your face.
It stops you from speaking
Prevents you from eating
And sends your emotions all over the place.

If love is listening,
polishing until glistening,
it would probably say to you:
'You are in love
There is nothing you can do.'

Love is a feeling that cannot be felt.
Its heat may be stifling
But its glaciers don't melt.
It will always leave you smiling.

It will always leave you smiling.

Love Mist

POSTCARD

The problem is that I never tell you
    the way I feel about you.
So I'll send you this card
    to show my loving regards.

LOVE ON THE LAKE

I know that we should be together
    in any kind of weather.
We should be together forever
Life would be much better.

I know that we should marry
    but I am in no hurry.
Though I do not want you to worry
There is no date in my diary.

Just being with each other
    is enough, as my lover.
And I hope you will discover
    one day as a mother.

We are here in the boat,
    on a lake that's so remote.
This place is like a moat
    and our love is still afloat.

Come on board with me today.
In my heart, you will always stay.
Like a gust of wind in early May
These are the feelings I convey.

I only hope this will last forever
Understanding our pain and pleasure.
And we will always be together
Through all the pain and pressure.

SHAKY LOVE

You have got my heart in a flutter.
My hands shake so much I can't spread butter.
So I send this shaky letter saying 'I love you'.

Writing this to you makes me feel so much better.

LOVE, CHILDREN AND LIFE

I guess we have to do it again.
In many ways it feels so mundane.
Yet it is so easy to explain.
If not done you really feel the pain.

One day a year we celebrate
    with our nearest and dearest.
Snatching time to be intimate
    after children has to be quickest.

It is incredible what flowers and cards can do
With a bit of champagne to relax the mood.
Then feelings run high and a kiss or three,
before our child shouts out 'Mummy!'

Then it is time for bed
And a chance for love there instead.
Waiting for the moment and counting sheep
By the time we've got around to it,
We've fallen fast asleep.

FORBIDDEN LOVE

I've got the idea in my head
That you keep your love unsaid.
You may hide it behind a door
Maybe in a kitchen drawer.

But not in your heart
That tears you apart.
Wherever your love is kept,
As long as I am there, I accept.

VALENTINE SURPRISE

I went to my mother with this dismal tale.
I said that I was sad; I never received any mail.
No one ever wrote to me. I felt that I had failed.
Why doesn't anyone write to me, even in Braille?

She said, 'If you want a letter every day
You'll need stationery and a stamp to pay.
Then post yourself a letter without delay.
From then on you will get one daily.
That should make you feel happy, greatly.'

I listened to what my mother said.
I understood it clearly in my head.
I sent myself a letter without delay
And looked forward to the post next day.

When the postie put the letter through my door
I picked it up right off the floor
Opened it up and what a surprise
A letter from me before my eyes.

Then I thought, how about a Christmas card?
Never getting one is very hard.
What about Easter and my birthday?
I craved a card from my dream Valentine love.
I thought that was crazy, so I prayed to the above.

The card arrived the following morning
Unsigned but so heartwarming.
My unrequited love lights were burning.
My internal combustion churning.
I had a card, I held it close to my heart.

Four years later two Valentine cards appeared.
I said to myself, something must be wrong
On Valentine's Day, love is for one.

I went to my mother in disbelief.
Why had two cards had been sent?
I asked her what that meant.

My mother took me aside
Knelt beside me and said:

'Valentine's Day comes once a year
When men propose to the love they hold dear.
Every fourth year women have the right to decide.
On a leap year a woman can propose to a man.
Not only have you sent yourself a Valentine of love,
But you also want to marry yourself. Lord above!'

My mother sighed.
'Don't do this again,
more than one love in your life is insane.'

FLO

There was a young lady called Flo,
Who loved me so much, don't you know?
    When she reached out to kiss me,
    Unfortunately she missed me
And now her lips are stuck to the floor.

BRAY

There was a young man called Bray
Ladies swooned over him all day
'I don't mind the feelings you display
But even though it's Valentine's Day
Remember, I'm gay!'

LOVE TRIBUTE

I hop, skip and jump
When you tell me you love me
And want to stay wth me
Forever and a day.

The world keeps spinning
So many sounds are in my head.
Please tell me what you found
As we lie here on the ground.

As the days just slip away
And we lie here in the hay
Getting ready for a brand-new day
What do you expect in early May?

In the fresh morning air
The sky is blue and clear
And we are still free.
You will always be with me.

Where do we go from here?
We love each other that's clear.
As we change through the gears
our love will last through the years.

COME BACK

I missed you so much when you left.
It made me so sad and bereft.
If I could only tell you that I'm sorry,
That I want you back in a hurry,
Then my life would be without worry.

OH JOY

You have got a hold on my every word.
Like no one else you rock my world.
Oh joy, you have my mind in a whirl.
Like a pearl in a love tale I see unfurl.

You attracted me with your eyes,
Shining with your bright-eyed smiles.
With enough light to make anyone cry
Without knowing the reason why.

Your complexion reminds me of a fine wine
From the restaurant where we always dine.
You have nothing more to refine.
The best thing is that you'll always be mine.

You won me with your voice, unlike any I'd ever heard.
With your golden hair and the way you stare.
Oh joy, you got my mind in a whirl.
You're the most beautiful joy I have in this world.

Your touch sends shivers down my spine.
As a person you're so kind.
Your poise and confidence are so refined.
Our lives together will be sublime.
There is no one else I want to be with.

I don't know what to say but 'Gee Whizz'.
And I have so much more to give
To enjoy each other as long as we live.

You won me with your voice, unlike any I'd ever heard.
With your golden hair and the way you stare.
Oh joy, you got my mind in a whirl.
You're the most beautiful joy I have in this world.

MARRIAGE?

Let me propose to you today
By writing my offer on this card.
I have never felt this way.
Will you marry me on Valentine's Day?

MY VALENTINE'S CHOICE

'We should wed,' she said.
'It's a Leap Year,' she said.
'And it is my choice.
A day to rejoice.'
I said I would marry
But I'm in no hurry
There's no need to scurry.
'Ask me in four years instead,'
I said.

POSTBOX

I reached the postbox just before five.
The postie had yet to arrive.
I popped the card into the box
In time for the postman's drop.

It was the last post before Valentine's Day.
How lucky I was, I have to say,
To send a card to my loved one.
My work for the day had been done.

WHAT?

I got a card for Valentine's Day!
It was not signed, as far as I could see.
I did not know it was a Valentine's card.
Unfortunately, I cannot read.

LOVE

After what we've been through
We are so glad we have you.
And if all the things we say are true
Only love and happiness can grow.

We may not always say the things we feel
And many times we seek to conceal
What we really feel about each other
And hide under a blanket cover.

I just want to say
We love you all anyway.
In good times and bad
Whether happy or sad.

Today we nearly reached the end
But we got through as we're all friends.
And though we never mean to offend
Sometimes we fail to understand.

We stuck together and made our plan
As the only way we could get out of this jam.
When you're in the furl or dip
We had to think. There was only one trick.

I just want to say
We love you all anyway.
In good times and bad.
Whether we're happy or sad.

Now we can all live forever
With each other at our leisure
We'll say nice things together.
It's love and happiness lasting forever.

When all things are said and done
We have had so much fun.
All we want to say about love
Is that you cannot get enough.

I just want to say
We love you all anyway.
In good times and bad.
Whether we're happy or sad.

I just want to say
We love you all anyway.
In good times and bad.
Whether we're happy or sad.

Love

A BARD'S REPLY

Shall I compare thee to a summer's day?
  Nay, try again in winter when thermostats are in play.
Thou art more lovely and more temperate:
  Your beauty from your mother, did you inherit?
Rough winds do shake the darling buds of May,
  But tempers fray with each passing day.
And summer's lease hath all too short a date;
  When the sun goes down before eight.
Sometime too hot the eye of heaven shines,
  My ardour gets softer in the cold winter times.
And often is his gold complexion dimm'd;
  I'll get under the sunlamp. Let's begin.
And every fair from fair sometimes declines,
  Meaning love may fade over time.
By chance or nature's changing course untrimmed;
  And as light passes, the night begins.
But thy eternal summer shall not fade,
  'Til winter arrives and snowmen are made.
Nor lose possession of that fair thou ow'st;
  Except with ice-cold underwear up to my chest.
Nor shall death brag thou wander'st in his shade,
  Don't worry. I'll find another, so don't be dismayed.

When in eternal lines to time thou grow'st:
>It gets much colder when the clouds snowest.

So long as men can breathe or eyes can see,
>I'll go to Specsavers, I'll guarantee.

So long lives this, and this gives life to thee.
>A Happy Valentine to you and me.

GONE

I was angry that you didn't send me a card.
I don't know why I was being so hard.
You sent a card each and every year.
Then I realised you were no longer here.

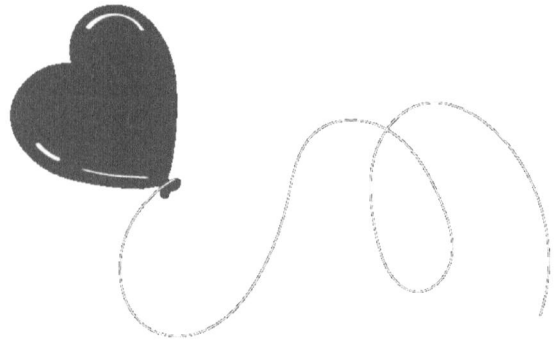

TRUE LOVE

I said I would love no other.
I have told you I am no bluffer.
That I would never look for another.
You said, 'I should think so. I am your mother.'
Happy Valentine's Day, Mum!

MAY I ASK YOU YOUR NAME?

I know they say everyone is the same
The difference is just a spectrum if you wish to blame.
So I ask this question to add fire to the flame
'May I please ask you your name?'

I guess you know why I'm asking
I spent a lot of time just thinking
About who you are.
Have you come from afar?
And if from your universe, what star?

If only I had the nerve.
I know I have the urge
To enquire, maybe just mention,
or speak out and ask the question.
Your name?
That would be a sensation.

HIDDEN LOVE

I hide my love under a Bushell.
So no one can tell
My feelings about you.
For your love I did fall.

VALENTINE GIRL

I have so much to give
And so much life to live.
I am like a dove.
I am in love.

I'll get out of bed.
It's my day ahead.
I'm not going to cry
There's a card nearby.

I think it's from you
And you'll be over before two.
We've even chosen the ring.
They say love grows in early spring.

I'll take a shower.
We won't quarrel.
I'm happy and glad.
Tears fall but I'm not sad.

Today, I have so much to do.
I'm so grateful, it is true.
As for the future,
Here's the thing,
Where's the proposal?
God only knows what that will bring.

Will you sing or get down on one knee?
Offer the ring or ask to be set free?
Which, to me, makes perfect sense
As I'm feeling rather tense.
Please don't leave me in suspense.
Don't worry about cost
Don't spare any expense.

One way or another it's a great day for me.
Betrothed for life or being set free.
I'll only know in an hour or so.
Whether to marry or to let go.

LOVE BITES

Oh, love bit me where it hurts
In both my head and my heart
But that pain was full of wonder.
Love was so much fun when I was younger.

WOW, WOW, SHE LOVES ME

When I first saw you I was making a pitch.
Your kind of look was making me twitch.
I don't know what it's all about
I only know I want to sing and shout.

You came over to me and looked me in the eye.
I came over queasy and felt like I was gonna die.
She said, 'Boy, you're the one I'm looking for.'
The next thing I knew was that I was on the floor.

    Wow, wow, she loves me.
    Wow, wow, I'm on a jet ski.
    Wow, wow, oh god she met me.
    Wow, wow, it's my destiny.

    Wow, wow, she loves me.
    Wow, wow, I'm on a jet ski.
    Wow, wow, oh god she met me.
    Wow, wow, it's my destiny.

I stood up tall and looked back at her,
When I tried to speak, it was almost like a purr.
Then I whistled and stuttered, my words began to
    slur
Then my world crumbled to a blur.

I tried to compose, get my legs straight.
Fell back over and ended up prostrate.
I looked around; everyone was laughing
While I lay there sputtering and coughing.

   I was dreaming.

   Wow, wow, she loves me.
   Wow, wow, I'm on a jet ski.
   Wow, wow, oh god she met me.
   Wow, wow, it's my destiny.

   Wow, wow, she loves me.
   Wow, wow, I'm on a jet ski.
   Wow, wow, oh god she met me.
   Wow, wow, it's my destiny.

Then I woke up from my dream
Everything was what it seemed.
Lying next to me was the girl of my dreams.
But I was now awake; we are a team.

My mad dream told me how lucky I was.
I married the girl who stole my heart.
In the dream I couldn't believe my luck.
Tongue-tied and prostrate with incredible love.

And I kept thinking.

Wow, wow, she loves me.
Wow, wow, I'm on a jet ski.
Wow, wow, oh god she met me.
Wow, wow, it's my destiny.

Wow, wow, she loves me.
Wow, wow, I'm on a jet ski.
Wow, wow, oh god she met me.
Wow, wow, it's my destiny.

Wow, Wow, She Loves Me

TOGETHERNESS

You love me. You love me,
I always said we would tie the knot.
With all our love and affection
We had made that connection.

Oh, to hold hands together.
So much love to last forever.
Right through 'til the twelfth of never.
Can any feelings be any better?

You're in my heart and in my soul
And being together is my goal.
We want all the world to know.
Let the storms rise, let the wind blow.

Our feelings are inseparable.
Each and every day, incredible.
Whether silly or sensible,
Erratic or incomprehensible.

I think I know how this will play out
Without the need to pray aloud.
To be who you are and I'm in no doubt
Isn't that what life is all about?

You're in my heart and in my soul
And being together is my goal.
We want the world to know.
Let the storms rise, let the wind blow.

Being together, whatever the weather,
In both sun and rain,
We will always remain.
Being together, whenever, wherever.

Just like heather and feather
Always pictured together
Whatever the weather.

You're in my heart and in my soul
And being together is my goal.
We want the world to know.

You're in my heart and in my soul
And being together is my goal.
We want the world to know.
Let the storms rise, let the wind blow.

LOVE A-PLENTY

Valentine's love I have plenty.
My feelings for you leave me empty.
To have so much love gets me through.
Especially if that love is without you.

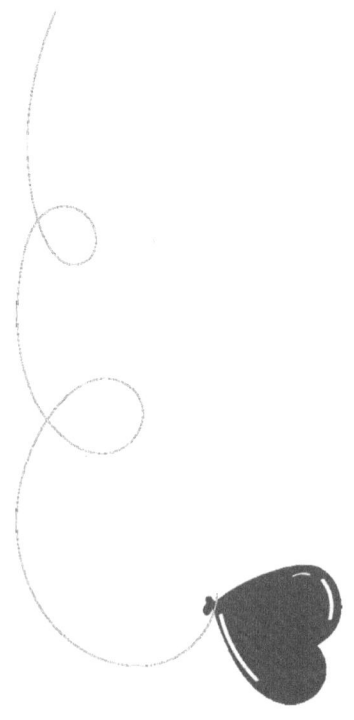

BRAILLE

I received a card in Braille.
When you're sightless, there's nothing else.
I could tell the depth of feeling.
My touch reading was so revealing.

EMPTY

So empty is my life without you
I don't know what to do.
Each day I sit alone and cry
Asking myself the reasons why.

There are no reasons, you said.
You just needed to clear your head.
If there's one thing I would change
It's for you to come back to me again.

HOW TO MAKE A VALENTINE CAKE

Have ready 125 g /4 oz unsalted butter softened
Squish about until it feels like cotton.
Then mix 125 g /4 oz caster sugar
Envelope it until it looks mature.

Add in 2 free range eggs
and stir until they sit up and beg.
Pour in 125 g /4 oz self-raising flour
until it looks good enough to devour.

Fill with 150 g /5 oz of raspberries
Although individual tastes may vary,
With passion fruit, sieved and pulped,
Adding in love as a result.

Pour in a little milk
Make the texture like silk.
Mix it in, you're in for a treat.
Set the oven at 180 (350) heat.

Cook for about twenty minutes,
Somewhere around those limits.
Take it out and cool it for ten.
Spread the icing – to your liking.

Mingle 500 g/1 lb 1½ oz of icing sugar
With 160 g/5½ oz of butter
But don't turn it into rubber.

Then add in the flavour filler
Of a seed pod of vanilla.
Trickle in drops of pink food colouring
Add in milk for a bit of bulking.

Whisked together for your pleasure
Licking your fingers in the measure.
Then sprinkle hundreds and thousands
On your delicious cake mountain.

When the cake is moist
You can then rejoice.
Although it takes some time to make.
It will be your very own Valentine bake!

BALLENTINE VALENTINE

I come from Ballentine
And for the very first time
A letter came through the letter box.
It gave me such a shock.
Handwritten, it said, 'I love you, My Valentine.'

SPICE UP YOUR LIFE

Oh, Valentine, should I be kind?
I want to give you a gift.
Something you would have as a wish.

Flowers, candles and kisses are fine.
Maybe a bottle of continental wine?
Or should I be more avant-garde –
perhaps matching underwear and a low-cut bra?

A variety of yogurts, je ne sais quoi?
Or luxury fondues with toxic alcoholic allures?
I know what you're thinking, and so am I.

Strangely, I spend all year thinking, why
Should I be doing this just this day for my wife?
When we have three hundred sixty-four days to
   spice up our life.

KISS

One more, just one more kiss.
What can I take from this?
I pray to the Lord above
That your kiss is made of love.

MY VALENTINE

I met this girl Val.
I had known her for a time.
I asked what her surname was.
She asked why.
I said, 'Just because.'

She told me,
'My name is Ms. Val Entine.'
I asked her if we could get together
I wanted her to be my Valentine forever.

THE LOVE–HATE GAME

I thought you hated me
Conflated and debased me
Deflated and defaced me
I thought you would meat-grind me.

You didn't like my hair
Or the clothes I had to wear
My shoe style was all wrong
My manner was headstrong.

Then one day you sent me a card
Apologising for being so hard.
You thought the only way to get my attention
Was to pick up on and mention
The traits that I had
Which were really not that bad.
Some criticisms were only inventions.

I apologised – so bizarre –
For not being good enough to tell
That I had good points as well.

I said, 'I can't help being like my dad.'
You flung your arms around my neck.
You kissed me. I hit the deck.

I stood up and proposed.
You did not say no
But, 'Yes, I suppose.'

We married soon after
And lived a life of laughter
About the ways
You treated me in those days.

So don't take comments as they're said
There may be an underlying motive instead.
The next time they treat you with disregard
Send them a Valentine's Card.

VALENTINE'S JEST

I knew there was something I had to do.
An event that would make you so happy today.
So I sent you a birthday card on Valentine's Day.

With a bottle of beer to apologise, but hey!
I thought I was being a little bit funny
But you didn't and threw me some money.

Then you drank the beer
Said, 'Get out of here
I never want to see you again.'

From the next Valentine's joke, I refrain!

FEBRUARY FROLICS

Oh, the weather's on the change.
The snow has lost its range.
Children are out playing their games.
As the days draw out
There are a lot of people about.

Birds begin to sing – is this the start of spring?
The sun comes out and for a moment spring
 appears.
I'm sure I heard a lawnmower changing gears.
And they say that love is in the air,

A walk will take you out and about.
Relief that winter has passed without doubt.
They say this lovely weather will last.
For mid-February the weather has surpassed.

Yellow and white flowers begin to bloom
Charting the end of the winter gloom.
Bringing along the darling buds of spring
And whatever else the new season brings.

Well then I get a card.
It got me right here in my heart.
Someone loves me and it's true
I guess that someone is really you.

WHOOPIE!

When I go out for a walk today
I'll greet people, turn and say,
'Isn't it great to be alive?'
My hopes and dreams still survive.
It's a time for flowers, cards and champagne
As it's Valentine's Day once again.

ST VALENTINE'S NIGHT

I'm looking for love in the late night.
I'm looking until the first dawn light.
I know that tomorrow will bring
Cards, flowers and romantic bling.

Saint Valentine shine on me
I feel lucky in a romantic way.
I hope my luck will hold and stay,
Until my love makes my day.

St Valentine pray for me.
I need love and want to be free.
I can't help the way that I feel.
I know these feelings are right.
Bring me love here overnight.

Find me someone who knows wrong from right
From the night until first light.
Let them be free to love me for a while
Then walk away in style.
Love me till they can't love again
And then keep going until the very end.

When love turns into sensual pain
When love is life's only full gain
Then we will turn it over and start again.
St Valentine make love your refrain.

I need love and want it for me
I can't help the way that I feel
I know these feelings are real.
St Valentine, pray for me.

I need love and want it for me
I can't help the way that I feel
I know these feelings are real.

The night is over and I haven't had a kiss.
St Valentine I'll give you a miss
Until next year I'll wait with anticipation
Then I'll return for Valentine's sensation.

LOVE IS LIKE A CARDBOARD BOX

Love is like a cardboard box.
It holds, well, quite a lot.
It can be packed up to the brim
Until it spills over when you put more in.

Then it explodes and scatters its contents
The good and the bad as a consequence.
So don't hold your love in one place
As it hurts too much to replace.

ST VALENTINE'S MASSACRE

A Canadian came walking by
He looked over and gave me an eye.
I asked if he was an expat.
He said yes and stopped for a chat.

He was over here on leave
He enjoyed travelling overseas
And loved the British ladies.
I thought to myself, well maybe.

He talked about life at home
Where buffalo are free to roam
Where temperatures dip below twenty
Saying it was the promised land of plenty.

I told him of my life
Troubled background full of vice.
I thought my criminal background would suffice
To be a gangster moll with a knife.

Oh that's not bad, he said
The worst thing that can happen is that you'll be dead
Then you won't need to worry about tomorrow
Though you will leave behind plenty of sorrow.

I asked him to be my Valentine.
He said yes but it may take time.
He would have to think about it, he said,
I took out a gun and shot him in the head.

NOTICE

I must have been born under a rock
Not to see you and take a second look
You took my breath away.

    What else can I say?

NEIGHBOUR

I feel that I am
   the man
      for you
         but I am shy.

I don't know why
   but it makes me cry.

That doesn't mean
   I am feeling
      less for you.

If we could get together
   anytime
      anywhere
         whatever.

As long as the answer is not
   'not ever'.

My feelings are so strong
That it would not take long
Before I announce to the world
That the girl I adore
Is married to the man next door.

LOVE IS AN OPEN DOOR

Love is an open door.
Open wider, you can have more.
But too much love will hurt you
The door will close and desert you.

Love is an open door
Don't let it slam in your face.
Always remember what love is for
As losing it leaves a nasty taste.

Love is an open door
Listen closely and I'll tell you more.
Ignore it and you're on the floor!
Embrace it, and it's everything you've ever asked for.

I say

>Love is an open door
>Love is an open door
>Love is an open door
>Love is an open door.

Love is an open door
Step in and you'll want some more.
You'll see there is more in store.
It'll steal your heart to the core.

Love is an open door
It's something you can't ignore.
You can't cast it aside or build a wall
It is there once and for all.

Love is an open door.
Believe me I'm back for more.
It's a feeling that's worth revealing.
Otherwise what are we all here for?

I say

> Love is an open door
> Love is an open door
> Love is an open door
> Love is an open door.

Love is an Open Door

NAMELESS

I didn't know your name
I was in love with you all the same.

I could send a Valentine's card, unsigned.
I'll find out your name another time.

COMMUNICATE

I was sitting on the lavatory
Thinking about the tragedy
Of my unrequited love for you.
There is no one else. It's true.

So I thought I'd drop you a line
To say that I was feeling fine
That I missed you very much
And that I wish you the best of luck.

I addressed all my feelings for you.
My love of all the things that you do.
I couldn't tell you I was in a mess.
So if you can, could you send me your address?

I realised you would not receive
This letter of love. I felt relieved.
I really did feel so small. Then I remembered
I had your number. I would give you a call.

OH DARLING

Oh Darling
 you are so startling
 and to my liking.

You're so striking
 that's why I'm writing
 you are so exciting.

I tell you this is true
 three simple words
 I Love You.

A YOUNG MAN FROM LISKEARD

There was a young man from Liskeard
Who sent his heart in a Valentine's card.
    When the girl opened it up
    She knew he was rough
As he had written his name inside.
Now, she'll never walk down the aisle as his bride.

VALENTINO

I've sent so many Valentine cards
To all the woman I have ever known.
I never receive a return.
I guess I will never learn.

The moral is to have a love for none.
Think of heaven, then minus one.
When she doesn't reply
Don't worry, she loves another guy.

I WISH

I wish I'd loved you when I could.
Showered you with flowers from Willow Wood.
A floral splay of my deep, proud emotions
With the petal sand roots of my devotions.

PAINFUL

I thought I could send a card,
After all it's not that hard.
I didn't think you had another,
I just thought you loved no other.

It was returned the other day.
On the card it sadly said,

> 'You were once the only one
> Now I'm free and having fun
> So save your cash and your time
> All I can say is, I'm doing fine.
> Send that card to someone who cares
> As living with you was too much to bear.'

GOODBYE

Today I woke up and cried
You were no longer by my side
Although you said you would leave
It was the last thing I ever believed.

LOVE IS A FOUR-LETTER WORD

Let me talk about this word called love.
Let me tell you it is no bluff.
Before you no Valentine passed my way
Now my emotions have set me free.

Love is a four-letter word
Tweeting like an early morning bird
Skewing my head and blurring my mind
Like a storm blowing in the wind.

   Oh, la, la, la.
   Oh, la, la, la.

Love is an intense feeling of affection
An emotion that flies in your direction
Loving all your imperfections
And follows on in life's reflections.

Four letters make a word
Some say it is absurd
That so many emotions are stored
In you, the person so adored.

   Oh, la, la, la.
   Oh, la, la. la.

Love is a four-letter word
Tweeting like an early morning bird
Skewing my head and blurring my mind
Like a storm blowing in the wind.

    Oh, la, la, la.
    Oh, la, la. la.

Love is a Four Letter Word

E-CARD

I looked at the floor
Nothing there at all
I was sure you would send me a card.

But as the postman walked by
He looked kind of shy
Did he know the reason why?

The next day
In case of delay
I looked again for that card
Nothing was there; I found this hard.

So I dropped you a line
To say I was fine
But missed your Valentine.

You replied saying check your mail
And if that fails
Look in junk
Where it may have well sunk.

I asked did you get my card.
You said, 'Yes but in that regard
You failed to put a stamp on it handsome
I resented paying the postman's ransom.'

You said, 'I sent your card back
With a note saying the post was not paid
Now our love will be delayed.'

I LOVE YOU

Dibble, dabble, dibble, dob,
Scooby, doobie, do.
Say it out and be proud
But more importantly say this loud:
I Love You

ONLY YOU

I was lonely
I felt like the one and only
With no love in my life
Until you came along.

I felt so proud I said out loud,
You have the aroma of Devon.
I looked to the clouds to clear any doubt
As I knew you were sent by heaven.

It's nice to be loved by everybody
Much better than being loved by nobody
But I would always be askew
If I were only loved by you.

It's bad to be lonely
When you're the one and only
And if you are beside yourself
You may be left on the shelf.

So don't despair
Someone is there.
As simple as one and one is two
There is someone there for you.

WAITING FOR LOVE

You're so nice
    like an oriental spice.
And you have the grace
    of a movement in space.

Slowly gliding along
    as a crooner sings a song.
So, never let it be said
    that love is dead.

Just wait until it comes along.

TRY A LITTLE TINDERNESS

Oh, you may be weary
Loving with no tenderness.
So when you get weary
Try a little Tinderness.

PRICELESS

Though we don't have a penny
Possessions not many
We don't get down.
We just about swim, not drown.

No, we don't drown.
We don't eat out, or get about.
Having little reserve
We have what we deserve.

But we are happy.
Nothing will stop me
Showing you my devotion.
No assets, but pure emotion.

Money and possessions in love are nice
But they are not what makes love alight.
It is our expression of how we feel
That is what I can reveal.

OUR SONG

Do you remember our song
That we loved and was just for us?
May our song always sing to you
And the words and emotions remain true.

LOVE BIRDS

Tweet, tweet, stay on your knees
Kiss my hand and say this if you please.
That you love me and will always be mine
Today and forever, to the end of time.

Our nest is our home
And we will never roam.
Nestling the young ones
Until their wings have flown.

We are joined together like birds of a feather
So willing to work together.
Love-struck and withstanding life's pressures
Like table salt standing with pepper.

CERTAIN NOTHING

You've got that certain nothing
Not a thing that I would need
But without that certain nothing
Our love would not succeed.

WORK AND PLAY

I work with my hands
That's what makes me a man
But when I get home to you
So much love makes me new.

We hold hands when making our meal
Not having to say how or what we feel.
It is part of who we are
That we will not stray too far
From each other.

We only need ourselves
To watch the wind and set the sails
For where we are going
Feeling the love that is growing.

Love grows with each passing eve.
When I get home I never want to leave.

Until it is time for bed.
Then we kiss and say goodbye.
Sleeping through the night.
Seeing each other tomorrow tonight.

OLD CROC

From one old croc to another
You're past your sell-by date
But before they make me a handbag by Pierre Cardin
If I knock on your door, will you let me in?

LITTLE BY LITTLE

Step by step
Stride by stride
Toe by toe
Millimetre by millimetre
Our relationship grows.

No seismic shifts
Tectonic drifts
Tornado storms
Or massive bee swarms.

We grow so slowly that it's hard to see
But does it matter to anyone other than you and me?
It's better to have two steps forward and one step
  back
Than two steps back, in fact.

No one else can see
How our love has to be
Behind the scenes
With our hopes and dreams.

Slowly and gradually laying the foundations
For long relations on all occasions.
Building the structures for our life
That's how we become man and wife.

I'M LOOKING OUT FOR YOU

I've got your back.
I've got your front.
I'm at your side.
I bear the brunt.

I'm so square with you.
Your sniper and your guru.
I write your lines.
I'm looking out for you.

I'm looking out for you
So you can be assured
A lifetime of happiness, no regrets,
There is nothing I will ever forget.

I'm looking out for you
So you can be assured
Of a lifetime of happiness with no regrets.
There is nothing I will ever forget.

From the time to get up
Until it's time to go to bed
Everything is done for you
Even your emails are read.

I answer your calls
Take care of it all
So you can be you
I am at your beck and call.

I'm looking out for you
So you can be assured
A lifetime of happiness, no regrets,
There is nothing I will ever forget.

I'm looking out for you
So you can be assured
A lifetime of happiness, no regrets,
There is nothing I will ever forget.

I do this for you,
For you, this is true,
So that forever and ever
I'll always be with you.

Love makes me do this
With you at home to kiss
My life is full of bliss.
It's an honour, I insist.

I'm looking out for you
So you can be assured
A lifetime of happiness, no regrets,
There is nothing I will ever forget.

I'm looking out for you
So you can be assured
Of a lifetime of happiness with no regrets.
There is nothing I will ever forget.

I'm Looking Out for You

CRYPTO

You are more than money to me
Your crypto cash is an ode to joy rhythm
And while I'm no Al Gore fan
I love your algorism

HOT LOVE

I am thinking of you
Getting into a stew
If only you would discover
How my love for you boils over.

ROLO LOVE

Would I give you my last Rolo
Or let you suck the middle of my Polo?
Would that be brave or maybe naïve
Or is it just true love?

If you had no money to go to the match
And you said, 'Please, I have a need'
Would I hand over the cash
Knowing I'll never get it back?
Is that true love or am I fool?

Accepting love as a tool
Allowing your feelings and emotions
To give you the notion
And confirmation of your true love.

It does not matter at all.
In the end it is your call.
It is only you who can see it through
And prove that love is true.

FANTASTIC

If I were Barbie and you were Ken
Would you love me even if you are not quite a man.
It's fantastic that we're made out of plastic.

EXPLAINING

I cannot describe
Your beauty. Besides
I am not one to brag.
Though I confess that I have
Someone I can call my own.
Now I will never again be alone.
Knowing what you are like on the inside
I take this with a shed full of pride
Your beauty is also seen on the outside.

EVERYTHING

I feel it in my heart
As I have felt it from the start.
Whenever we are together
Whenever we are apart.

I feel it in my soul
In my being, in my whole.
A sense so intense
That I never feel alone.

I feel it in the ether
It has top spot on my meter.
I cannot compete as you are the elite
Of everything I ever wanted you to be.

SPRING LOVE

Some love is internal
Another can be fraternal
Mothers are always maternal
Fathers paternal
Love is best vernal
As love springs eternal
To get it I keep a journal.

OWED TO LOVE

As a baby in my mother's arms
I felt loved and safe from harm.
As I grew I felt safe and secure
As I grew, I knew I needed more.

Though my love needs were altered
Your love for me never faltered.
Independence comes with age
And there comes a time to turn the page.

    We are owed to love
    We are bestowed, bestowed with love.
    We are betrothed with love.
    We are resolved with love.

As I grew older
With responsibilities on my shoulder
Love needs included financial support
And my teenage needs for transport.

Then I found my first love
So many hormones waiting to bud
Emotions flowing from my head
And I asked my love to share my bed.

> We are owed to love
> We are bestowed, bestowed with love.
> We are betrothed with love.
> We are resolved with love.

We stayed in love for the rest of the time.
Four children, three of which are mine.
I gave them the love my parents gave me
From holding them close to sat on my knee.

Until they grew up
And had children of their own.
Now we live alone. On our own.
Love has flowed through our veins
Until the cycle of love begins again.

> We are owed to love
> We are bestowed, bestowed with love.
> We are betrothed with love.
> We are resolved with love.

Owed to Love

TOMORROW

Today I feel sad
Today I feel bad
But tomorrow I will be glad
I think you will understand

I DREAM

I dream of you each night
Every day you are in my mind
I can't get you out of my head
You're in every book I've ever read.

Your name is in every song I've ever sung
Gripped on a climbing a ladder, each and every rung
In every picture I've ever hung
Wherever I am you belong.

My dreams are sweetness and light
Getting me through each and every night
And in my head they always stay
Each and every day.

My dreams have taken life
My future's looking bright.
When you said let's stay together
Until the twelfth of never
I knew everything will be alright.

MISSING YOU

I miss you so much
I am so grateful for your love
It hurts that you walked away
I hope you come back one day

I JUST WANT YOU TO STAY

If I knew how to be me
    I'd be.
But now
    I find that I don't know.

Maybe I will find a way
To see what to do
To be free of these feelings of pain
    And of loss again.

If you could feel my pain.
Am I going insane?

Whatever it is,
    will this?
But now I am so alone, alone, alone.
Just come home
Just for a day
I just want you to stay.

If I knew how to be me
    I'd be.
But now
    I find that I don't know.

Maybe I will find a way
To see what to do
To be free of these feelings of pain
    And of loss again.

If you could feel my pain.
Am I going insane?

Whatever it is,
will this?
But now I am so alone, alone, alone.
just come home,
just for a day,
I just want you to stay.

I Just Want You to Stay

WARMLY

Warmly, stunningly, sunningly. breezily
Shades of weather I associate with thee.
Cold, bitter and freezing
Are these shades associated with me?

But when we are together
We discuss the weather
Snuggle up together
Never showing displeasure.

COINED

I am smitten by you
What can I do?
Can you unlock your spell
Or throw a coin in the well?

MY LOVE

You are my love
Sent from above
From the galaxy of my mind
Universal interstellar time.

I know of no other lover
Who could make me uncover
The feelings you give me.
You can be set on it and call it love.
It makes you weak at the knees
And go out of your way to please.

You feel really happy inside
Like a paper plane watch it glide.
My love has no sense.
My life is intense.
Not just monumental but immense.
Let the love shower commence.

My love is a true love
Only seen once in a lifetime.
I'll grab it while I can
And think how lucky I am.
Miss it and it may never pass again.

SONG FOR LOVE

If only I knew what to say
I would do it without a delay.
So I have to be strong
And say I love you in a song.

A song for love to last a lifetime
For you and me, for all time.
Sung with rhythm and with rhyme
Let the church bells chime.

I'll sing a song for love, my love
It feels so good when you are near
It's a feeling I can't explain
Over and over and over again.

We climb the ladder of love each day
Some days we have nothing to say
Though in our hearts we are one
And will carry on until our lives are done.

A song of love doesn't need many words
Despite what you hear, nor what you've heard.
With music lifting our hearts
When we're in love we're never apart.

I'll sing a song for love, my love
It feels so good when you are near
It's a feeling I can't explain
Over and over and over again.

I no longer need to sing my love for you
Words can't explain how we feel; it's true.
You were right when you remarked,
'Love only works when it hurts your heart.'

I'll sing a song for love, my love
It feels so good when you are near
It's a feeling I can't explain
Over and over and over again.

Song for Love

SAYING

I said that I'll always love you
And still to this day that is true.
I want the world to know
The feelings I hold.
As the saying goes
What you reap, you sow.

MY FRIEND

You are my friend from beginning to end,
Sharing our smouldering embers of fun.
Turning like a Ferris Wheel in the breeze,
Knowing that our friendship will survive.

Love turns and changes over time.
From solid feelings to being together, being
  together.
Sharing the burdens of planning our futures,
Enjoying each other's sense of humour.

We spend our time at leisure.
It's a pleasure, in equal measure, love.
In life, a life lived without pressure,
You're my friend, my heart, my treasure.

Fending off offending vultures,
When children come along.
And responsibilities wear us down,
It is friendship and teamwork that gets us through.
And that is shared with me and you.

When bills and finances get you down.
And we can't afford to paint the town.
As there's no money left to pay the loan.

We spend our time at leisure.
It's a pleasure, in equal measure, love
In life, a life lived without pressure,
You're my friend, my heart, my treasure.

After years, still side by side
Debts cleared; kids spread wings wide
Together, in this life's ride"

We spend our time at leisure.
It's a pleasure, in equal measure, love.
A life without pressure,
You're my friend, my heart my treasure.

NO PROBLEM

You love me; yes, you do.
I love you; yes, I do.
We love each other
That also is true.

Everything about our love – I feel good –
All your bad points are understood
And all my good points reassure me
As each day passes I want you more.

It is true we have bad days and good
But our love is as solid as wood
And the bad times are just splinters we fix
Picking them off to use as toothpicks.

There are no problems we cannot solve
As we both have a mutual resolve
We do not need to have others involved
As we effervesce until dissolved.

Life has its ups and downs
And we have occasional frowns
We can count them on one hand to amount
But there is no problem we cannot surmount.

PETAL

Love is like a violet petal
soft and silky, in fine fettle.
An aroma to touch the perfect palette
with a taste of a terrific word salad.
Or a simple taste of an old-time ballad
croaking like a duck-billed Mallard.
If that is a thought, that is valid.

But it is not tragic
Maybe a tad magic
Perhaps a little elastic
Expanding in the heat
Before twanging back in defeat.

Love is everything and nothing if
No one really understands it.
Just like a petal on a flower
It cannot stand without a leaf
Underneath.

And a stem that acts as a stilt
That will not wilt
But the aroma from a petal
Will help that love light settle
With a flower as my vessel.

All I can say is
Love is like a violet petal
soft and silky, in fine fettle.

ABOUT THE AUTHOR

John Eaton is a poet and song writer, also a nurse and care home manager. He lives and works in Taunton, Somerset, UK.

John started writing during lockdown as a means of staying sane, keeping in touch and building a relationship with his granddaughter, Evaleigh. He has always had an affinity with the English language, and space and time provided the opportunity to create. He is passionate about encouraging literacy and a love of language.

When John left school, he did not know what, if anything, he should be good at. As one of eight children and growing up on a council estate he did not aspire to a higher purpose. Working in a psychiatric hospital, qualifying as a Mental Health Nurse (RMN) and then as a Registered General

Nurse (RGN) led him overseas, then to establishing a successful healthcare training business and subsequently a growing care home in Somerset.

John's work is inspired by the people, punishment, pathos and humorous proclamations he encounters in his day job.

His first collection of poems, *Thoughts from a Faraway Place,* was published in 2021 (Austin Macauley). Thus far, John has written and produced a dozen Spid the Spider books, three albums and many other songs, including 'Under Ukrainian Skies' to support the Ukrainian relief effort. The music was composed mostly by Pete Dymond, Dymond Studios.

Listen to musical versions of his work at https://soundcloud.com/john-eaton-205933369 and all good streaming services.